RACIAL JUSTICE IN AMERICA

What Is

WHITE PRIVILEGE?

LEIGH ANN ERICKSON WITH KELISA WING

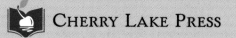
CHERRY LAKE PRESS

Published in the United States of America by Cherry Lake Publishing Group
Ann Arbor, Michigan
www.cherrylakepublishing.com

Reading Adviser: Marla Conn, MS, Ed., Literacy specialist, Read-Ability, Inc.
Content Adviser: Kelisa Wing
Book Design and Cover Art: Felicia Macheske

Photo Credits: © FS Stock/Shutterstock.com, 5; © VGstockstudio/Shutterstock.com, 6; © sirtravelalot/Shutterstock.com, 9; Library of Congress/Photograph by Warren Leffler, LOC Control No.: 2003673965, 11; Library of Congress/LOC Control No.: 2007676238, 13; © Monkey Business Images/Shutterstock.com, 19; © Mega Pixel/Shutterstock.com, 20; © Billion Photos/Shutterstock.com, 20; © Quang Ho/Shutterstock.com, 20; © Dee Dalasio/Shutterstock.com, 23; © Rawpixel.com/Shutterstock.com, 25; © vasara/Shutterstock.com, 27; © Lissandra Melo/Shutterstock.com, 30; © Pavel1964/Shutterstock.com, 31

Graphics Throughout: © debra hughes/Shutterstock.com; © GoodStudio/Shutterstock.com; © Natewimon Nantiwat/Shutterstock.com; © Galyna_P/Shutterstock.com

Names: Erickson, Leigh Ann, author. | Wing, Kelisa, author.
Title: What is white privilege? / Leigh Ann Erickson, Kelisa Wing.
Description: Ann Arbor, Michigan : Cherry Lake Publishing, [2021] |
  Series: Racial justice in America | Includes bibliographical references. | Audience: Grades 4-6 | Summary: "Race in America has been avoided in children's education for too long. 'What Is White Privilege?' explores the concept of systemic and intrinsic racism in a comprehensive, honest, and age-appropriate way. Developed in conjunction with educator, advocate, and author Kelisa Wing to reach children of all races and encourage them to approach race issues with open eyes and minds. Includes 21st Century Skills and content, as well as a PBL activity across the Racial Justice in America series. Also includes a table of contents, glossary, index, author biography, sidebars, educational matter, and activities"— Provided by publisher.
Identifiers: LCCN 2020039995 (print) | LCCN 2020039996 (ebook)
  | ISBN 9781534180239 (hardcover) | ISBN 9781534181946 (paperback)
  | ISBN 9781534181243 (pdf) | ISBN 9781534182950 (ebook)
Subjects: LCSH: Racism—United States—Juvenile literature. | Privilege
  (Social psychology)—United States—Juvenile literature. | Race
  awareness—United States—Juvenile literature. | United States—Race
  relations—Juvenile literature.
Classification: LCC E184.A1 E7735 2021 (print) | LCC E184.A1 (ebook) |
  DDC 305.800973--dc23
LC record available at https://lccn.loc.gov/2020039995
LC ebook record available at https://lccn.loc.gov/2020039996

Cherry Lake Publishing Group would like to acknowledge the work of the Partnership for 21st Century Learning, a Network of Battelle for Kids. Please visit http://www.battelleforkids.org/networks/p21 for more information.

Printed in the United States of America
Corporate Graphics

Leigh Ann Erickson has taught in New York City, Chicago, rural Ohio, and Mt. Vernon, Iowa. She aims to eradicate racism through justice driven curriculum. Erickson is founder of Undone Consulting and The Undone Movement, a nationwide movement of racial reconciling. Grateful to play a small role in centuries long resistance work, she owes much to her family, friends, and mentors.

Kelisa Wing honorably served in the U.S. Army and has been an educator for 14 years. She is the author of *Promises and Possibilities: Dismantling the School to Prison Pipeline*, *If I Could: Lessons for Navigating an Unjust World*, and *Weeds & Seeds: How to Stay Positive in the Midst of Life's Storms*. She speaks both nationally and internationally about discipline reform, equity, and student engagement. Kelisa lives in Northern Virginia with her husband and two children.

CHAPTER 1

What Does White Privilege Look Like?

Imagine you're at the starting line of a race. Your heart is beating fast. You feel nervous as you wait to begin. You look up and down the starting line, sizing up the competition, wondering if you have enough speed to outrun them. Suddenly, an official steps into the middle of the track and tells the runners that obstacles will be placed in each person's lane. "Okay," you think, "that's kind of exciting." A crew of people come out with the obstacles.

As you look around, you notice that the obstacles being placed in the other runners' lanes look different than yours. You see high fences, large pools, mud, and barbed wire. In your lane, you see a row of hurdles that you've been taught to easily leap over. The other runners look confused. You are confused. How is it possible that your race will be so easy and their race will be so hard?

How is White privilege like a track race with unfair obstacles?

What you are experiencing in this moment is called privilege. Privilege is defined as a special right or advantage *granted* to one particular person or group. The word granted is an important part of the definition. Privilege is not something that is earned; it is *granted*, or given.

What are some things that may make it easier for White students to

There are a lot of different types of privilege that exist in society for a lot of different reasons. In the United States, racial bias and racism have led to something called White privilege. White privilege means that because of ongoing biases and racism in people and the places they work, White people have more access to power and resources than a Black, Indigenous, or Person of Color (BIPOC) in the same situation.

The phrase "in the same situation" is very important. For example, a White upper-class middle school student living in New York City will usually have more access to power and privileges than a Black upper-class middle school student. What do some of these powers and privileges look like? Books that these students read feature mostly White characters. (Around three-quarters of all children's books published in 2018 were about White people.) Students learn U.S. history from the perspective of White people. (A study by the Southern Poverty Law Center found that only 8 percent of graduating seniors believed that slavery was a main cause of the Civil War. It was.) White students are also more likely to be placed in advanced classes and are less likely to be suspended or arrested in school. Those things can make a big difference in people's lives!

Did you know that a Black boy who grows up in a wealthy community has a much greater chance of living in poverty as an adult than a White boy does? That Black boy may be just as smart and talented and may work just as hard as his White friend, but the Black boy may have more obstacles in his path that make gaining wealth more difficult. He may face racial discrimination when he tries to purchase a home or apply for a job. His White friend may have to overcome obstacles, but they will not involve racial discrimination, which means his friend has White privilege.

Sometimes, to understand what White privilege *is*, it's helpful to understand what White privilege *is not*. White privilege does not mean that White people have never worked hard. It does not mean that White people have not earned some of the success and power they have. It also does not mean White people have never suffered.

On Your Mark, Get Set, GO!

Think about the race mentioned at the beginning of chapter one. What are some ways the race is fair? What are some ways it is unfair? Then think about your own school. Do lanes look different for different people? Explain. How can you work with your classmates to create a fair race for everyone?

Think about this story. My great-grandfather was White and a coal miner in the 1920s. He worked long hours in the mines, earned very little money for his family, and suffered a lot. He got very sick from breathing in coal dust. The good news is, he also had the opportunity to work his way up to higher-paying jobs in the mines, build his own home, and raise a family.

Life for Black coal miners was usually different because of racism, discrimination, and few laws to protect them. The majority of Black coal miners worked the hardest and most dangerous jobs in the mines and received the lowest pay. All of this put more obstacles in place, preventing them from living a prosperous life. My great-grandfather worked hard and also benefited from his White privilege.

White privilege hurts a lot of people. If you are Black, you might have experienced this hurt, and it might make you angry or sad. If you are White, you might feel bad about hurting others or you might feel afraid to lose this privilege. You feel these things because White privilege is bad for everyone, including White people. That's because White privilege is the result of centuries of racism and bias.

There is hope! By learning more about White privilege, we can work to spend it, end it, and build a country where everyone has the opportunity to run—free of unfair obstacles and to the best of their ability.

Critical Thinking

In 1965, President Lyndon Johnson gave a speech promoting the passing of the Voting Rights Act. This important legislation prohibited racial discrimination in voting. Johnson said, "You do not take a man who has been hampered by chains for years, release and lead him to the start of a race, saying 'you are free to compete with others,' and still justly believe that has been completely fair."

President Lyndon Baines Johnson signing Civil Rights Bill, April 11, 1968.

CHAPTER 2

Where Did White Privilege Come From?

Now you might be thinking, "Hey, wait a minute, doesn't everybody in the United States have the same opportunities? When slavery ended, didn't Black people become totally free?" Thinking this is technically right, but there are a lot of ways Black people have been prevented from accessing these rights. To understand a little better, let's travel back in time to an era called Reconstruction (1865–1877). During this period, attempts were made to fix inequalities caused by racism and slavery.

When slavery ended, three amendments were added to the U.S. Constitution giving Black people the same rights as White people. The 13th Amendment ended slavery. The 14th Amendment gave Black people the right to be an American citizen. The 15th Amendment gave Black men the right to vote. Black people also could now earn a paycheck, own land, and receive an education. For a little while, this worked. In fact, during Reconstruction, 1,500 Black leaders were voted into power. Some Black families that had been broken up because of slavery were reunited, and Black people began building free lives across America.

A family stands in front of the former slave quarters of the Hermitage Plantation, Savannah, Georgia, 1907.

Tragically, many White people, who had spent centuries enslaving Black people, did not like the power that Black people now had. These White people tried to take that power away. One organization that did this was the Ku Klux Klan. This hate group, which still exists, formed after the Civil War. It used violence to force Black people from their homes and jobs and to prevent them from voting. Reconstruction ended with the U.S. government unable to protect the rights of formerly enslaved people. Beginning in the 1870s and lasting until the 1960s, strict Jim Crow laws made segregation legal. This made it harder to get jobs, houses, and an education. It was a violent era. In fact, between 1882 and 1968, there were nearly 5,000 recorded lynchings of Black people in the United States, and many more lynchings likely went unrecorded. Many call this an era of racial terror.

Laws passed during the civil rights movement ended legal segregation in the 1960s. However, a lot of White people in power didn't want to follow the laws that were passed. When the United States passed a law saying that Black and White children must be allowed to go to the same public school, some states closed all of their public schools. White students in these states got money to go to private schools, and Black students were left without a school for several years.

Spend Your Privilege!

Privilege is like extra money in your pocket that you didn't earn. How we use, or spend, that extra money matters! Joan Trumpauer Mulholland is a White activist who spent her privilege. During the civil rights movement, she was a Freedom Rider who protested segregation on buses throughout the South. She was hunted by the Ku Klux Klan and spent time in prison for breaking segregation laws. She saw that the world she lived in was unjust and worked to change it. She now runs an organization that educates young people about the civil rights movement and how to become activists in their communities.

You might be asking yourself, "Why would White people do this?" The answer lies in understanding what racism is. When the United States became a country, the people in charge had to create laws for its citizens. The people in charge were White, and most of them believed that Black people should be enslaved. They believed that Black people didn't deserve the same rights and freedoms as White people because they didn't see Black people as their equals. This is racial bias. This belief came from many places, including inaccurate descriptions of Africans and African culture from people who had traveled to the continent. And it came from a desire by White people to build wealth using the free labor that enslaved people provided.

Racism happens when racial bias leads to action. The actions that the people who founded this country took and the laws that they created deeply hurt people who were not White. That hurt continues today. White privilege and the advantages that come with it are the result of racial bias and racism.

It's important to remember that White privilege is not the end of the story for Black people. Black people have not just walked away from the starting line because they looked down at their lane and saw the obstacles in their way. Throughout history, Black people have powerfully resisted racism, bias, and White privilege, and have overcome many obstacles. At the end of Reconstruction, Black people lost their homes and their jobs, so they built their own towns! The Jim Crow era was violent and unfair, so some Black people moved north to search for a better life. Some stayed in the South and fought to build their lives. When Black people saw how unfair segregation laws were, they stood against them and changed them during the civil rights movement.

Today, Black and White people around the nation see that things still aren't fair. Together, they are marching for new laws and more freedoms for BIPOC people in the United States and around the world!

You can learn a lot about the civil rights movement by visiting the United States Civil Rights Trail online. Go to the website *https://civilrightstrail. com* and compare what was happening during the civil rights movement to what you see happening today in the Black Lives Matter movement. What rights are people asking for? How are they making sure they get those rights?

CHAPTER 3

White Privilege Today

White privilege still exists today. It's easy to spot when you know some of the disparities in this country. In 2019, White workers who went to college earned over $10,000 more per year than Black workers who went to college. In 2016, schools with mostly White students received $23 billion (yes, you read that right) more per year than schools with mostly Black students. These kinds of differences give White people more power and more White privilege.

Hanging on to White privilege hurts BIPOC in the United States. Even though laws in our nation aren't overtly discriminatory, life is still not fair for BIPOC. Many laws are written with White privilege. This means that it will be easier for White people to follow the law and White people will get privileges because of the law.

New Perspectives!

Interview a friend who is different than you in some way. Ask your friend what their life is like. What are some wonderful things they experience? What are some challenges they experience? Practice being a good listener while your friend talks. Then switch! Ask your friend to interview you.

Surrounding yourself with diverse friends will lead to a richer life.

Peggy McIntosh
The First Person to Define White Privilege

In 1988, Peggy McIntosh was the first person to define White privilege in her article "Unpacking the Invisible Knapsack." She asked herself, "On an everyday-basis, what do I have that I didn't earn?" She came up with 46 examples of White privilege. Some examples included going into a store without being followed, not being singled out by police, and seeing people like her in movies, magazines, and books. What are some examples of White privilege that you see in your life?

For example, there is no law stating that police should arrest Black people more than White people. Yet Black people are more likely to be stopped, arrested, and killed by police officers than White people. This is true even though the same number of White and Black people commit crimes. When stopped and questioned by police, studies have shown that White people are more likely to receive the benefit of the doubt than Black people are. Black people may need others to back up what they say in order to be believed. These are examples of dangerous White privilege that many in our nation are trying to end.

Another example is school dress code policies. These rules about a person's appearance often impact a Black person's culture and style. For example, some schools say students can't wear dreadlocks or multiple barrettes in their hair. This rule affects Black students since they are more likely to wear their hair this way. One student, DeAndre Arnold, challenged this rule in his Texas school. DeAndre refused to cut his dreadlocks, explaining that his hair was part of his family's tradition. His family is from Trinidad. Many people believed that DeAndre should be allowed to keep his dreadlocks. His school, however, suspended him and would not allow him to attend his graduation.

This is an example of a rule that impacts Black students more than White students. And it's another example of White privilege.

These examples might make you feel discouraged, but don't give up hope. It is an exciting time! Many people are saying the laws and policies that create White privilege should be changed. Protests are happening around the country, and many organizations are asking for change. In schools, students are asking for new dress code policies, classes, and books that represent all people. White people who understand their privilege are using it to help remove obstacles that might prevent BIPOC from achieving success.

White Privilege in My World

Find a copy of your student handbook. Are there any rules or policies that might discriminate against BIPOC and give advantages to White students? Analyze the handbook for bias and White privilege. Discuss what you find with your classmates and teacher.

The spring and summer of 2020 saw thousands of protests for equality around the country—and world.

DO THE WORK!

ESSENTIAL QUESTION

How can we be anti-racist?

Becoming anti-racist requires actively working against racism using words and actions. This project-based learning assignment will allow you to practice these skills. Read all the books in the *Racial Justice in America* series. Through each "DO THE WORK!" activity, you will research and put together parts of a larger project that will allow you to grow and help others grow as well.

What parts of my identity have provided me with privilege? How can I use my privilege to help others? Part of understanding our privilege is understanding ourself and others and how to use our privilege to bring about social justice. For this portion of your project, you are going to identify what makes you who you are by creating an identity map. Ways people identify are by their gender, race, religion, ethnicity group, interests, military affiliation, family, and many other things. How do you identify? What makes you who you are? Creatively display your identity wheel, chart, or list. Identify things that have given you a privilege or a disadvantage. Address how your identity can help you to achieve racial justice.

For the presentation of your final work, you can create a collage, magazine, podcast, jigsaw puzzle, poem, video, or social media campaign—anything to demonstrate your learning. No matter what you do, just be creative, learn something new, and publicize your work!

CHAPTER 4

Taking Action

You might be wondering, "What can I do?" That is a very good question. If you are a student of color who is reading this, be encouraged. Look to your history and your community for ways to resist and stand against racism. Know your rights and learn how to use them. There may be obstacles in your path, but continue to work, like those who came before you, against those obstacles.

If you are a White person reading this, there are several steps you can take to end White privilege. First, understand that White privilege isn't good for anybody, even you! It does not feel good to have a lot of things that you didn't earn when other people don't get to have those same things. It does not feel good to see your Black friends or their families be less safe and have less opportunities than you do. When you are staring down that track, it might be exciting to think you're going to win the race because there are less obstacles in your way. But will you really feel good at the end of the race when you look back and see others fighting obstacles that you didn't even have? Instead of taking off down your path, what if you helped take away the obstacles in other runners' paths? Then they could join you in this great race of humanity.

Overcoming White privilege is a job that must start with the White community insisting on fairness and equality across all races.

where to START?

1. DON'T BE COLOR-BLIND: Telling yourself or other people that you "don't see color" isn't true and isn't fair. We need to make sure we see *all* of who a person is. Then we can see *all* of what that person might be going through—the good and the bad. When you see color, you see more of what makes that person who they are. Be careful, though. Do not *only* look at color. Race is one part of a person, but it is only *one* part. There are many, many parts that make up a whole person.

2. LISTEN: One effect of White privilege is that White people may believe that racism isn't as bad or as harmful as it really is. That's because they haven't experienced it personally. When you hear people talk about racism or an experience they have had with racism, listen and believe them.

3. UNPACK YOUR BACKPACK: This is a popular phrase that means to think about all the advantages you have every day because you are White. Think about other people, in your same situation, who are not White. Imagine yourself spending the day as they do. Imagine yourself walking in their shoes. What do you have that they don't? Doing this helps you understand what other people are going through. When you see all that you have been given, it will be easier to have compassion for other people and not judge them.

4. PASS ON YOUR PRIVILEGE: Unpacking your backpack will help you see all the things you have that you can *give* to help others *gain*. It is a privilege (honor) to spend your privilege (tools you were given) to help others. Fannie Lou Hamer, a Black woman who worked very hard during the civil rights movement, said, "Nobody's free until everybody's free." Spending your privilege to help take down the obstacles in other people's paths is freeing. Did your Black friend tell you he was treated unfairly by the teacher? Ask him if he wants you to go with him to talk to the teacher or the principal. Do you see a White person saying racist things to a BIPOC in the hallway? Go over there and say that it's wrong and tell an adult. Is there a protest for equality and justice happening in your community? Ask a family member or trusted adult to take you.

Understanding Privilege

On April 5, 1968, the day after Dr. Martin Luther King Jr. was murdered, a White third-grade teacher knew she had to do something different with her mostly White class. The teacher, Jane Elliott, taught her students about racism and privilege. She divided up her class according to eye color and gave different children advantages and disadvantages based on their eye color. Each child got to experience both sides. Years later, during interviews with these students, they said this lesson was a life-changing experience. Think of another way you could teach others about White privilege that will help them understand and make them want to work for change.

Martin Luther King Jr. Memorial in Washington, D.C.

Now that you know about White privilege, you can do something about it. Let's get working so we can all get running!

Pushing yourself to stand against White privilege can be uncomfortable, but it is essential for a more fair society.

Collins, Cory. "What Is White Privilege, Really?" Teaching Tolerance, Fall 2018, Issue 60. www.tolerance.org/magazine/fall-2018/what-is-white-privilege-really.

Cracking the Codes: Joy DeGruy. "A Trip to the Grocery Store." YouTube, September 20, 2011. *https://www.youtube.com/watch?v=Wf9QBnPK6Yg*.

Privilege Aptitude Test. From the National Civil Rights Museum at the Lorraine Motel (n.d.). *https://assets.speakcdn.com/assets/2417/Youth-PrivilegeAptitudeTest.pdf*. Accessed August 28, 2020.

Brown, Cynthia Stokes. *Refusing Racism: White Allies and the Struggle for Civil Rights*. New York, NY: Teachers College Press, 2002.

Stevenson, Bryan. *Just Mercy: Adapted for Young Adults: A True Story of the Fight for Justice*. New York, NY: Delacorte Press, 2018.

GLOSSARY

activist (AK-tuh-vist) a person who fights to bring about political or social change

civil rights movement (SIV-uhl RITES MOOV-muhnt) the national effort made by Black people and their supporters in the 1950s and 1960s to eliminate segregation and gain equal rights

culture (KUHL-chur) the ideas, customs, traditions, and way of life of a group of people

discrimination (dis-krim-uh-NAY-shuhn) the unfair treatment of others based on differences in such things as race, age, or gender

disparities (dis-PAIR-uh-teez) great or large differences

era (ER-uh) a long period of time in history that has some consistent feature

Freedom Rider (FREE-duhm RYE-dur) a person who refused to follow racial laws in the American South in the 1960s that required segregated seating on buses

Jim Crow (JIHM KROH) the deeply unfair treatment of Black people in the United States through laws that kept them separate from Whites

lynchings (LIN-ch-inghs) illegal executions of a person by a mob of people

racial bias (RAY-shuhl BYE-uhs) a belief that one race of people is superior or inferior to another

racism (RAY-siz-uhm) unfair treatment of people based on the belief that one race is better than another race

Reconstruction (REE-kon-struck-shun) the reorganization of the South after the Civil War

resources (REE-sors-iz) people, places, or things you can turn to for help or support

segregation (seg-rih-GAY-shuhn) the practice of keeping people or groups apart

unjust (uhn-JUHST) unfair; morally wrong

upper-class (UHP-ur KLAS) a social group that has the highest status in society typically because the group is wealthy

INDEX